THE RUDE MOOSE

By JENNA LAFFIN

Illustrated by TINA KUGLER

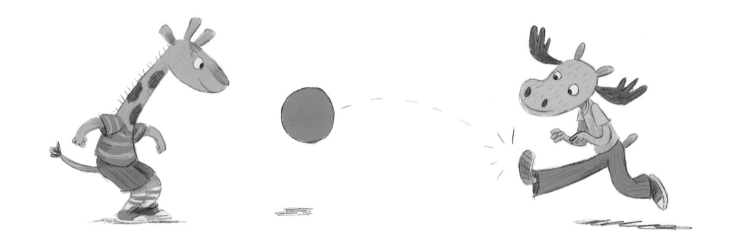

CANTATA
LEARNING

MANKATO, MINNESOTA

WWW.CANTATALEARNING.COM

CANTATA LEARNING
MANKATO, MINNESOTA

Published by Cantata Learning
1710 Roe Crest Drive
North Mankato, MN 56003
www.cantatalearning.com

Library of Congress Control Number: 2014956993
978-1-63290-257-3 (hardcover/CD)
978-1-63290-409-6 (paperback/CD)
978-1-63290-451-5 (paperback)

The Rude Moose by Jenna Laffin
Illustrated by Tina Kugler

Book design, Tim Palin Creative
Editorial direction, Flat Sole Studio
Executive musical production and direction, Elizabeth Draper
Music produced by Wes Schuck
Audio recorded, mixed, and mastered at Two Fish Studios, Mankato, MN

Printed in the United States of America.

VISIT
WWW.CANTATALEARNING.COM/ACCESS-OUR-MUSIC
TO SING ALONG TO THE SONG

Good manners are important. Using them shows other people that you care about them and their feelings. Using good manners with other people also makes the time you spend with them more **pleasant**.

Now turn the page,
and sing along.

There once was a moose
that everyone called **rude**.

He never used his **manners**. It's true!

When it was time to line up,
he would always **budge**.

The other animals tried not
to hold a **grudge**.

9

When the others talked,
he didn't wait his turn.

Since he was always talking,
it was hard for him to learn.

Sometimes the moose said "sorry" with a **sneer**.

But everyone could tell that he wasn't **sincere**.

There once was a moose
that everyone called rude.

He never used his manners. It's true!

16

One day the frog said, "That wasn't very nice!"

The moose felt sad and said, "I'll apologize."

"I cared only for myself,
and that wasn't right.

18

I'll be kind, at least I'll try,

for the rest of my life!"

19

There once was a moose
that everyone called rude
until he learned to use his manners.
It's true.

SONG LYRICS
The Rude Moose

There once was a moose
that everyone called rude.

He never used his manners. It's true!

When it was time to line up,
he would always budge.

The other animals tried not
to hold a grudge.

When the others talked,
he didn't wait his turn.

Since he was always talking,
it was hard for him to learn.

Sometimes the moose said "sorry"
with a sneer.
But everyone could tell he wasn't
sincere.

There once was a moose
that everyone called rude.

He never used his manners. It's true!

One day the frog said, "That wasn't
very nice!"

The moose felt sad and said, "I'll
apologize."

"I cared only for myself,
and that wasn't right.

I'll be kind, at least I'll try,
for the rest of my life!"

There once was a moose
that everyone called rude

Until he learned to use his manners.
It's true!

The Rude Moose

Jazz
Wes Schuck

Chorus

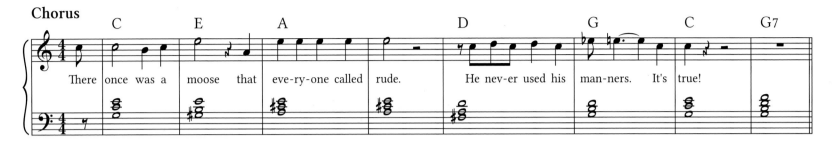

There once was a moose that eve-ry-one called rude. He nev-er used his man-ners. It's true!

Verse

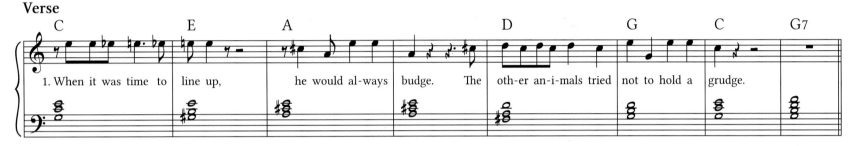

1. When it was time to line up, he would al-ways budge. The oth-er an-i-mals tried not to hold a grudge.

Verse 2

When others talked, he didn't wait his turn.
Since he was always talking, it was hard for him to learn.

Verse 3

Sometimes the moose said "sorry" with a sneer.
But everyone could tell that he wasn't sincere.

Chorus

Verse 4

One day the frog said, "That wasn't very nice!"
The moose felt sad and said, "I'll apologize."

Verse 5

"I cared only for myself, and that wasn't right.
I'll be kind, at least I'll try, for the rest of my life!"

Chorus

There once was a moose
that everyone called rude
Until he learned to use his manners. It's true!

GLOSSARY

budge—to unfairly cut in front of someone in a line

grudge—long-lasting bad feelings toward someone

manners—the way someone behaves around other people

pleasant—happy or enjoyable

rude—not showing other people respect

sincere—honest and real

sneer—to smile in a way that shows hate rather than kindness

GUIDED READING ACTIVITIES

1. What was the problem in this story? How was the problem solved?

2. How was the moose rude? What did he do?

3. Pick one of the rude things the moose did. Then explain how you would act differently if you were the moose.

TO LEARN MORE

Arnold, Tedd, et al. *Manners Mash-Up: A Goofy Guide to Good Behavior.* New York: Dial Books for Young Readers, 2011.

Boldt, Claudia. *You're a Rude Pig, Bertie!* New York: North-South Books, 2013.

Bracken, Beth. *Terrible, Awful, Horrible Manners!* North Mankato, MN: Picture Window Books, 2012.

Smith, Siân. *Manners at School.* Chicago: Heinemann, 2013.